BUS SCENE IN COLOUR:
LONDON BUSES 2000

Geoff Rixon

Ian Allan
PUBLISHING

Introduction

Welcome to *Bus Scene in Colour: London Buses 2000*, comprising a compilation of photographs depicting the current bus scene in London and its suburbs over the last few months or so, into the Millennium Year, 2000.

It is a timely look, as it covers a period which has seen major changes in the London bus scene itself, and it comes at a time when yet more change is imminent. For the first time in 15 years London is shortly to have an elected assembly and Mayor, and in July 2000 the Mayor will assume authority over London's transport. A new body called Transport for London is to be set up in July 2000, and though this was written only four months earlier there was no indication as to whether TfL would represent 'business as usual' or a whole new era.

The scene on the road has changed greatly too. Low-floor buses are now everywhere — including the new generation of double-deckers. At the beginning of the period covered by this book, the low-floor double-decker was a novelty; only 12 months later there were several hundred in service in London, built by DAF, Dennis and — just entering service in early 2000 — Volvo.

Despite the newcomers, the Old Faithful — the Routemaster — still provides solid and faithful service on the core of London's most demanding central routes, more than 50 years after the project to develop a new standard London bus to replace the trolleybuses had begun. Who on that original development team could have foreseen their new baby still providing front-line service in the next Millennium! How much longer the Routemaster will continue to serve Londoners is anybody's guess; a simplified fare structure was introduced at the beginning of the year, leading to much speculation that crew operation wouldn't last much longer. Indeed, with Smartcard technology coming along in about two years' time, more questions must be asked about the future of the Routemaster. However, at the time of writing we can still enjoy them, and whatever the speculation, there is little question of the Routemaster vanishing from the streets just yet.

In a most unlikely twist, London's bus history looked to be about to come full circle in early 2000. London Transport had finished privatising its bus services in 1995, but has suddenly found itself running its own buses again! London Transport had been pursuing a policy of trying to find smaller operators to operate routes, to prevent the larger groups having it all their own way and being able to push up prices. It was a policy which brought to the streets of London operators like Mitcham Belle and Wings of Uxbridge, but it also backfired more than once. The first time was on the infamous route 60 (see picture), but another smaller operator which London Transport had favoured with contracts was Harris Bus, of Grays, Essex. Unfortunately Harris found itself in the hands of official receivers, and no-one came forward to buy it — so London

---

Front Cover: Leaving the Millennium Dome, North Greenwich, on 27 January 2000 is MD11 (actually carrying fleetnumber 2011), one of 17 DAF SB220s with East Lancs Myllennium bodywork. These buses have been purchased by London Central for routes M1 and M2 to Charlton and Greenwich stations respectively. Three of the class are gas-powered, with storage tanks mounted on the roof. The guided busway, to be used by route M1, was not ready at the time of this photograph. *Geoff Rixon*

Back Cover: London General's RML2376 approaches Putney Bridge from Fulham Palace Road on route 14, still carrying out sterling work despite being exactly 34 years old when photographed in February 2000. This vehicle has had an Iveco engine for the past 10 years, and operates out of Putney garage, which has an allocation of 42 Routemasters for routes 14 and 22. Long may they continue. *Geoff Rixon*

Title Page: This scene, at Coulsdon, shows Capital Logistics' brand-new DAF/Optare Spectra, T125 AUA, apparently concluding an extraordinary saga which brought route 60 considerable press coverage for all the wrong reasons. Capital Logistics, having won the tender for the route, was scheduled to start operations in August 1998, but, because of delays in the delivery of new vehicles, several other operators had to step in to help out. Indeed, it was possible to find vehicles belonging to five different operators working route 60 on the same day. The Spectras are still used on the service, along with DAF/Plaxton Presidents, having passed to Tellings-Golden Miller which took over Capital Logistics on 1 June 1999. However, in a surprising move, Arriva London South took over the route from 4 March. *Geoff Rixon*

First published 2000

ISBN 0 7110 2763 3

© Geoff Rixon 2000

Published by Ian Allan Publishing

an imprint of Ian Allan Publishing Ltd, Terminal House, Shepperton, Surrey TW17 8AS.
Printed by Ian Allan Printing Ltd, Riverdene Business Park, Hersham, Surrey KT12 4RG.

Code: 0006/B2

Transport took the unusual step of taking it over. Will this remain a one-off situation, or does it mark a return to direct operation by London Transport itself?

It all goes to show that while we all like a bit of nostalgia, and to think back to the 'good old days', there is still never a dull moment on the London bus scene. The pace of change looks unlikely to slow in the new Millennium, and there are hopefully exciting times ahead, as the Deputy Prime Minister has allocated £50 million to improving bus priorities in the capital over the next couple of years.

Hopefully the photographs which follow will reflect some of the variety and change that has taken place over the last 12 months or so.

In compiling this album I should like to thank several friends for their invaluable help: Colin Brown, Dave Brown and Dave Drury for supplying some of their fine photographic material; Dave Stewart and Stephen Morris for helping with their extensive knowledge of vehicle facts and the London bus scene; Kevin McCormack for his many hours spent helping with the text and photographic selection, and Alan Stokes for his time carrying out the word-processing.

Geoff Rixon
East Molesey, Surrey
February 2000

Above: Standing outside the magnificent Grosvenor Hotel, Victoria, is Travel London Optare Solo 240, the last of a batch of 10 such vehicles delivered for use on route C1. These are the only Optare Solos used for bus work in London. *Colin Brown*

Left: The long-established, award-winning business known as Epsom Coaches returned to London bus operation in the autumn of 1997 when it took over routes 413 and S1 from London General. Using the branding 'Epsom Buses', the company now has some 50 buses operating on 13 routes. At the start of 1999, it took delivery of 11 new short (8.5m) Dennis Darts with Plaxton Pointer 2 bodywork. This view, at Grand Drive, Morden, shows S457 LGN on 5 January 1999. *Geoff Rixon*

Above: The prospect of a free service has failed to entice any passengers to travel on Airlinks' Dennis Dart/Plaxton Pointer 2 T71 WWV in this view taken in Viscount Way, Hatton Cross, on 27 March 1999. This was the second day of service with this type on route H30. *Geoff Rixon*

Left: Summer weather comes early to London in this view of a Big Bus Company Routemaster pulling away from St Paul's Cathedral on 31 March 1999. FPT 588C started life as Northern General 2118 in February 1965, and has been a regular performer on sightseeing duties for many years. *Geoff Rixon*

Right: The continuing introduction into London service of low-floor buses brought Alexander-bodied Dennis Tridents to the capital in January 1999, operating from Stagecoach East London's Leyton garage on route 55. TA45, on route 26 from Bow garage, was photographed turning out of The Cut into Waterloo Road on 16 March 1999. *Geoff Rixon*

Above: To mark the 20th anniversary of the retirement from regular service of London's famous RT class, Blue Triangle ran RT3871 on its route 127 (Tooting to Purley) for one day only. Looking remarkably short compared with today's buses, the RT takes what looks suspiciously like a full load of enthusiasts past the spring foliage of Mitcham Common, on 7 April 1999. Three days later, Blue Triangle relinquished this route to Mitcham Belle. RT3871 saw further public service in June 1999 when route 25 was transferred from Stagecoach East London to First Capital. *Geoff Rixon*

Right: A book covering the current London bus scene would not be complete without a red Routemaster, a type which is still playing a major rôle in Central London, having been pounding the streets for over forty years. This Arriva-owned example, RM1125, dates from May 1962 and is one of the standard Routemasters working alongside RMLs on Clapton's route 38. Now fitted with an Iveco engine, RM1125 is seen negotiating the roundabout at Hyde Park Corner on 31 July 1999. *Geoff Rixon*

Left: Capital Citybus became part of FirstGroup in July 1998, adopting the name First Capital. The first new vehicles to arrive under the new regime were 17 dual-door Volvo Olympians with Northern Counties Palatine I bodywork, which were put to work from 17 October 1998 on route 341 (formerly route 171A). Here we see No 215 travelling along London Wall in May 1999. *Geoff Rixon*

Above: The end of the century witnessed the resurrection of the 'DMS' classification, but these single-deck low-floor vehicles have absolutely nothing in common with the unfortunate Daimler Fleetlines of the 1970s except for the colour red! First CentreWest has adopted the Marshall-bodied Dennis Dart as the standard vehicle for Ealing Buses, either in longer, 10.2m form (DML) or, as pictured here, the shorter 8.9m type. DMS259 emerges from The Common (Ealing Common) outside The Grange Tavern on 14 April 1999, when the bus was just a few weeks old. *Colin Brown*

The successor to Blue Triangle on LTB tendered route 127 was Mitcham Belle, a coach company making its debut on the London bus scene; it obtained 12 new Dennis Dart SLFs, painted in patriotic livery, for the service. T156 OGC was photographed crossing The Pond in North Street, Carshalton, on 10 April 1999, the first day of operation. *Geoff Rixon*

London United has eschewed red and grey livery for Surrey County Council-supported Heathrow services, numbered 555/6/7. This view, taken in the attractive surroundings of Sunbury Village on 6 March 1999, shows Hounslow's Dennis Dart SLF DP29, with dual-door Plaxton Pointer 2 body, on its first day of service. *Geoff Rixon*

Left: Approaching London Bridge in July 1999, on Sightseeing Tour duty, is this monster belonging to London Pride Sightseeing of Rainham. The vehicle is MCW Metroliner C52 VJU, formerly with McGill of Gartocharn, near Loch Lomond, Scotland, and acquired by Ensign in 1995. *Geoff Rixon*

Above: F. E. Thorpe & Sons Ltd of North Kensington, which started as a small coach operator in the late 1960s, made its entry into the London Transport market in 1992 when it took over the London inter-station route. Having subsequently gained a large group of Mobility Bus routes in west and southwest London, the company moved into scheduled bus services in 1998 by winning the tender for route 210. A dozen dual-door Dart SLFs with Plaxton bodywork were purchased and decked out in an eye-catching livery of red and yellow, as illustrated by DLF30 at Brent Cross shopping centre in September 1999. *Geoff Rixon*

Left: Extra-long Routemaster JSJ 748, ex-LT RM80 and now ERM48, looks resplendent in its new livery as it passes St Paul's Cathedral on 31 March 1999. The Original London Sightseeing Tour is now operated by Arriva out of Wandsworth garage. *Geoff Rixon*

Above: The long-established Feltham to Heathrow Airport rail link was revamped in March 1999 when two new LTB contract routes were introduced (T123 to Terminals 1, 2, and 3, and T4 to Terminal 4). Operated by London United, the 11 Dennis Dart SLFs with Plaxton Pointer 2 bodywork are painted in a livery which is similar to Stagecoach South West Trains Class 442 'Wessex Electric' units. A solitary passenger enjoys a personal taxi service on 8 July 1999 as DP14 heads down Heathrow's Northern Perimeter Road. *Geoff Rixon*

The operation of Armchair's new Alexander-bodied Dennis Darts on route 49, starting from 28 May 1999, resulted from a complicated switch of services. The Darts were intended for route 209 (Hammersmith to Mortlake), which Armchair was to take over from London United. However, there was a delay in the raising of the weight limit on Hammersmith Bridge and the Armchair vehicles were too heavy while the lower limit was still in force. Meanwhile, route 49 was due to pass from London General to London United. Thus, until the weight limit was increased, London United continued to operate route 209 for a further five months while Armchair put its new Darts on route 49 for the same period. Here we see T148 AUA on its first day of service, proceeding along Kensington High Street. *Geoff Rixon*

The attractive colours of the familiar Grey-Green Volvo Citybuses which pre-
dated the 80%-red colour scheme edict are now just a memory. The company's
renaming as Arriva London North East has meant a return to red livery and the
operation of route 78 (Shoreditch to Peckham Rye), from November 1998, by
Alexander-bodied Dennis Darts. No 969 crosses Aldgate on 25 June 1999.
Geoff Rixon

Left: Limebourne, following a management buy-out from its former parent company, Q-Drive, as Independent Way Ltd, returned to operation of four routes (42, 156, C3 and C10) and went on to secure the 344 (Clapham Junction to London Bridge) in February 1999. T417 LGP, seen in Battersea Park Road on 28 June 1999, belongs to a batch of 34 Caetano Compass-bodied Dennis Dart SLFs. These vehicles are named after castles (the name is carried on the nearside, beside the entrance door) and have attractive dark green skirt panels. *Geoff Rixon*

Right: Leaving Romford station on 21 June 1999 is Blue Triangle's Metrobus MCW501, sporting the company's new livery. This route, 265, operates during Monday to Saturday shopping hours and is not to be confused with London General's Putney-Tolworth service of the same number. MCW501 was purchased from Yorkshire Rider earlier in 1999 but had only a short stay with Blue Triangle. *Colin Brown*

Left: Taken in Hertford Road, Lower Edmonton, on 11 September 1999, this could be a promotional shot for the low-floor bus, with wheelchair and pushchair waiting to board. The vehicle, Arriva London North DLA119, is a brand-new DAF DB250 with Alexander bodywork, operating out of Enfield garage on the long 279 route from Holloway to Waltham Cross. Eight of these vehicles operate alongside 20 Plaxton President-bodied DAF DB250s which are classified DLP. *Geoff Rixon*

Above: Entering Edmonton Green bus station in September 1999 is DLP6, contrasting with the dated appearance of the Metrobus (M765) behind. *Geoff Rixon*

Left: Arriva companies London North (formerly Leaside), London North East (Grey-Green) and London South (South London) operate from no fewer than 13 garages. This scene, at Camden Street in September 1999, shows L353, one of a batch of 40 Leyland Olympians with Alexander bodywork delivered in 1992. *Geoff Rixon*

Below: Capital Logistics, of West Drayton, was successful in May 1998 in winning LTB contract work when the company was awarded route U3 (Uxbridge station to Heathrow Airport). Nine new air-conditioned, double-glazed Optare Excels were used, painted in a striking red, white and blue livery. Capital Logistics also bid successfully for the former Green Line route 726 (replacing London Coaches), which also saw the new Optares from time to time running alongside the DAF/Ikarus Citibus fleet. R990 EWU was caught in Laurel Lane, West Drayton, on 8 August 1999. *Geoff Rixon*

Left: In order to fill in time between school journeys in the Ashtead/Leatherhead area, Nostalgiabus of Mitcham started operating scheduled services from Epsom, beginning on 13 September 1999. Three of the company's Routemasters received repaints during the year, and RM1394 makes a superb sight as it climbs Epsom Downs on 14 October 1999. Nostalgiabus has a varied fleet that includes representatives of the RF, RM, DMS and M classes, as well as ex-Merseyside Leyland Olympians. *Geoff Rixon*

Above: Travel London 404, photographed on 16 October 1999 at Parliament Square, belongs to a batch of 21 Optare Excels operating on route 211 out of Stewarts Lane rail depot. Travel West Midlands, part of National Express, obtained this service along with route C1 in mid-1997, and to operate them set up Travel London Ltd as a separate subsidiary within the group. *Geoff Rixon*

Left: The training fleets of several operators often seem to have more stunning liveries than the passenger-carrying fleets. This London General Metrobus, M1389, is no exception as it crosses Epsom Downs on 14 October 1999. *Geoff Rixon*

Right: Despite its picturesque setting, the terminus of route 161 at the War Memorial, Chislehurst, Kent, is on a busy road, and T405 SMV is waiting for a gap in the traffic before heading off to the Millennium Dome (North Greenwich) on 28 September 1999. The Dennis Trident with East Lancs Lolyne bodywork was one of 15 acquired by Metrobus in August 1999 for this route, shortly before the company was acquired by the Go-Ahead group. *Geoff Rixon*

Left: With Somerset House in the background, Arriva London South's L59 picks up on Waterloo Bridge on 6 October 1999. Recently outshopped, the vehicle is a 1986-vintage Leyland Olympian with Eastern Coach Works bodywork, and is based at Norwood garage. *Geoff Rixon*

Above: This Dennis Dart, DRN116, is one of five with Northern Counties Paladin bodywork which, having started life in 1994 with Kentish Bus, were then taken over by Grey-Green and now belong to Arriva London North, operating from Enfield garage. This view was taken at Edmonton Green in September 1999. *Geoff Rixon*

33

Left: Heading for Docklands on 16 October 1999 is TN863, one of 56 new Dennis Tridents with Plaxton President bodywork purchased by First Capital (Capital Citybus) for routes 1, 25 and W8. This shot of the premier route was taken at Waterloo. *Geoff Rixon*

Below: First Gold Arrow, operating from Westbourne Park garage, has done an excellent job in making RML2717 look as good as new in this view taken on 12 October 1999 west of Marble Arch. The remainder of the fleet used on route 23 have received the same treatment. *Geoff Rixon*

Left: Shortly after the total solar eclipse on 11 August 1999 — the first to be seen in mainland Britain since 29 June 1927 — SLD79 basks in the midday sun in Woolwich. This Stagecoach Dennis Dart with Alexander ALX200 bodywork is one of 48 delivered for the group's London operations in late 1998/early 1999, of which 30 were required by Selkent for routes 99, 178, 269 and 291. *Geoff Rixon*

Right: A freshly-painted Metrobus is a rare occurrence these days, now that large numbers have been displaced in London. However, several Metrobuses belonging to London United (Stanwell Buses Ltd) are allocated to the old Kingston garage for service on routes 411 and 568. In this view on 19 October 1999, M203 is travelling along Leatherhead Road, near Chessington World of Adventures, on a 568 working. *Geoff Rixon*

Left: London Central's route 36, worked out of New Cross garage, is one of the few still operated by the original standard-length Routemasters. Furthermore, the position seems unlikely to change for a few more years because, at the end of 1999, London Central successfully retained the route under the re-tendering process. We can now expect the more tired-looking RMs to receive some refurbishment to bring them up to the standard achieved by RM1305, seen here leaving Victoria station on 16 October 1999. *Geoff Rixon*

Above: For those who remember the scruffy RTs from Southall and Shepherd's Bush garages that soldiered on, working route 105 until the end of April 1978, the current scene is a world apart. Here, in Bath Road near the main entrance to Heathrow Airport, we see a Marshall-bodied Dennis Dart SLF, 643 in the fleet of London Buslines, based at Bridge Road, Southall. *Geoff Rixon*

Left: Metroline Travel was the first London operator to sample the low-floor Dennis Trident with Plaxton President bodywork, introducing the first 30 to Holloway's route 43 to replace MCW Metrobuses. Two further batches were then purchased for routes 17 and 134, increasing the class to 63 units. Having recently entered service, TP55 was photographed on 13 October 1999, loading up in the City Road, at Angel, Islington. At the time of going to press, Metroline had just been sold to Delgro, which also operates bus services in Singapore and Shanghai plus cabs in London. *Geoff Rixon*

Right: 1999 saw the return of Purfleet-based Ensignbus, and the company purchased a substantial fleet of secondhand Metrobuses from a wide range of operators. In this photograph, No 144 is entering the Bluewater shopping centre on its journey from Romford on 23 November 1999. A few weeks later, Ensign was taken over by fast-growing Town & Country Travel of Benfleet. *Geoff Rixon*

Left: TN849 picks up a passenger in Westbourne Terrace on 24 June 1999, its first day in service. The vehicle is one of 31 Dennis Tridents with Plaxton President bodywork purchased by First CentreWest to replace MCW Metrobuses on route 18, and operated by Westbourne Park garage. *Geoff Rixon*

Right: The Routemaster has received many different colour schemes throughout its lifetime but RM752, in British Tourist Authority multi-coloured livery, is certainly one of the brighter. Operating out of Wandsworth garage on the Original London Sightseeing Tour, this patriotic-looking vehicle, forty years young, stands at the lights west of Marble Arch on 27 July 1999. *Geoff Rixon*

Left: From 3 July 1999 the City branch of the Northern Line was closed for 10 weeks between Moorgate and Kennington. Extra buses were provided by London Central and London General, as part of the 133 route. This operation brought out Titans and Metrobuses, all seemingly in very good condition. It would be hard to find a more presentable vehicle than T172, from the Private Hire fleet, carrying tramway-style livery and seen at London Bridge in July 1999. *Geoff Rixon*

Below: Metroline Travel received 52 new Dennis Tridents with Alexander ALX400 bodywork between July and September 1999. Interestingly, these differ from the early Stagecoach deliveries in being shorter (9.9m instead of 10.5m) and taller (4.39m instead of 4.2m). With fleetnumbers following on from the TP class, the first 16 of these Tridents (TA66-81) went to Cricklewood for route 16, while the remaining 36 were sent to Harrow Weald for routes 140 and 182. TA89 had been in service for only a few days when it was photographed on 28 August 1999 at Sudbury. *Geoff Rixon*

Left: The Private Hire fleets of London General and London Central include three Metrobuses (OMs 171, 241 and 420) converted to open-top and painted in 'traditional' General livery. On 11 July 1999, OM241 was busy operating a park-and-ride service to the Hampton Court Flower Show, and was photographed in Walton Road, East Molesey. *Geoff Rixon*

Above: Tellings-Golden Miller of Byfleet, Surrey, is expanding rapidly, taking over local companies and various bus routes in areas to the west and southwest of London. One such route is the 465 (Teddington to Dorking) which Tellings took over following the closure of Leatherhead garage in May 1999. Still carrying London & Country livery is this 1997-built Plaxton Pointer-bodied Dennis Dart, seen arriving in Kingston on 29 July 1999 on a short working to Effingham. *Geoff Rixon*

Left: The Leyland Titan has proved to be a worthy London bus, with the class clocking up over 20 years of service. Although large numbers have been dispersed all round the country, the Stagecoach group still operates some 90 members of the class in London. This view shows T395 at Holborn Circus, substituting for an RML on route 8, complete with conductor! *Geoff Rixon*

Below: When the Go-Ahead group purchased London General in 1996 to add to London Central, it then had a London operation with over 1,000 buses. Between 1995 and 1998 Go-Ahead updated both fleets with 157 Volvo Olympians carrying Northern Counties Palatine I bodywork, creating the NV class. NV101-159 were delivered to Sutton garage for routes 93, 157 and 213, replacing Metrobuses; this photograph shows NV154 approaching Wimbledon on 27 July 1999. *Geoff Rixon*

Left: This scene dates from 10 July 1999 and features Upton Park's S31 at Ilford Broadway. The vehicle is one of two single-door Scanias with Northern Counties bodywork built in 1991 for London Buses and taken over by Stagecoach East London in 1994. S31 was used for a time on private-hire work from North Street, Romford, and was later transferred to Upton Park for use on route 147. In early February 2000, it moved to Stagecoach East Kent and now operates in Canterbury. *Colin Brown*

Above: Heading down the Marylebone Road in July 1999 is one of four Marshall-bodied Darts painted silver to match the Heathrow Express trains, with which they provide a link from various Mayfair hotels. The service was introduced in June 1998 and the vehicles belong to First CentreWest which has provided them with ex-Routemaster registration marks. *Geoff Rixon*

Left: Still going strong is 39-year-old RML891, one of 41 such vehicles operated by London United from Shepherd's Bush garage on routes 9 and 94. All have replacement Cummins engines and refurbished bodywork, although the company's two standard-length RMs still retain their AEC engines. This view was taken in Kensington High Street on 29 July 1999. *Geoff Rixon*

Above: During 1999 London United Busways received a large intake of over 100 Plaxton Pointer 2-bodied Dart SLFs, classified as DPs. Thirty went to Hounslow garage, displacing ageing Leyland Nationals on route H37 and earlier Darts and Leyland Lynxes on route H98. DP45 was photographed on route H37 on its second day of service — 10 July 1999 — in Hill Street, Richmond. *Geoff Rixon*

Left: As it travels along High Street, Kingston, towards its terminus on 28 August 1999, XL1 appears in excellent condition for a vehicle which has already seen two years of service. Stanwell Buses Ltd, part of London United Busways, has six Optare Excels, including XL1, which operate out of the old Kingston garage. The buses used on route 371 (Kingston to Richmond) all carry different slogans, referring to locations on the route. *Geoff Rixon*

Right: In 1992 nine Volvo B10M chassis dating from 1985 were rebodied by East Lancs as double-deckers for Grey-Green. Following the company's change of name to Arriva London North East, the vehicles were repainted into Arriva livery. Looking as though its rear has been sliced off, No 163 stands in traffic in Waterloo Road during March 1999, a few months before the Volvos were displaced on route 188 by new low-floor DAFs of the DLA class. *Geoff Rixon*

London Central and London General, both part of the Go-Ahead group, have large bus fleets which now include the ever-popular low-floor Dennis Darts with Plaxton bodywork. LDP128 is an example of the 10.1m version operating out of Merton garage on the Clapham Junction to Wimbledon 219 service; it was caught on camera in George Street, Wimbledon, on 28 July 1999. RF-operated route 219 from Kingston to Weybridge 'Vickers Works' is now just a distant memory from over 20 years ago. *Geoff Rixon*

Since the controversial withdrawal of Routemasters from Westbourne Park's route 28 in the spring of 1989, three different vehicle types have been used. The Mercedes-Benz midibuses were considered unsatisfactory and were replaced in the early 1990s by Wright Handybus-bodied Dennis Darts (DWs) carrying Co Antrim registrations. These were superseded in June 1999 by a new batch of Darts with dual-door Marshall 9.4m bodywork. Here we see First CentreWest's DM301 in Kensington High Street on 25 June 1999, shortly after its entry into service. *Geoff Rixon*

London Central DML23, belonging to a class of 29 Marshall-bodied Dennis Dart SLFs, arrives in Woolwich in August 1999 on route 244, its blinds already set for the return journey. The class is based at Bexleyheath garage for working routes 244 and 469. *Geoff Rixon*

In late 1997 Stagecoach Selkent took delivery of 18 Mercedes-Benz Vario midibuses — an unusual choice nowadays for a 'red' London bus operator — and classified them MB. Plumstead-based MB9 is seen in Woolwich, working route 380 in August 1999. *Geoff Rixon*

Left: London Traveller was formed in 1998, being a trading name of The Metropolitan Omnibus Co (London) Ltd, which is partly-owned by Yorkshire Traction. Operating from a base at Harlesden, the company obtained the 187 service (South Harrow station to Queen's Park station) from Metroline and started to operate it on 4 September 1999 using new Volvo B6BLEs with East Lancs bodywork. V504 EFR approaches Harlesden on 11 September 1999.
Geoff Rixon

Right: Sovereign Buses (London), owned by the Blazefield group, has a fleet of more than 100 vehicles and operates mainly in the Harrow area, apart from the RML-operated route 13 into central London. This view, taken in Shaftesbury Avenue, South Harrow, in October 1999, shows 1991-built Leyland Olympian H140 GGS wearing the recently-introduced Yorkshire Coastliner-style livery which is replacing the previous poppy red colour on all but the RMLs.
Dave Brown

Above: The Green Line name has been alive now for a remarkable 70 years and is carried here by Arriva East Herts & Essex (formerly County Bus & Coach) vehicle R208 VPU. This DAF SB220 with Plaxton Prestige bodywork is one of nine purchased new at the end of 1998 for the long-standing 724 service from Harlow bus station to Heathrow Airport, which is worked out of Ware garage. Shadows are lengthening in this shot at Kingston Lane, Hillingdon, on 16 November 1999. *Geoff Rixon*

Right: New to London Suburban Bus, an offshoot of a Liverpool independent operator, were 16 Volvo Olympians with Northern Counties Palatine II bodywork which arrived in 1993/4 and were put on to route 271. In April 1995 the company was taken over by MTL, the latter's London operations, in turn, being purchased by Metroline Holdings in 1998. Despite having had three different owners, the Olympians still operate route 271, and V203 is seen in Holloway Road in October 1999. *Geoff Rixon*

Where better to photograph one of Wing's buses than outside RAF Uxbridge! Wing's has been a luxury travel company for many years but ventured into buses for the first time when, from 13 November 1999, it took over former CentreWest route 207A. This view, taken on 16 November, shows one of the three new Dart SLFs with East Lancs Spryte bodywork purchased for this service, which has been re-routed and renumbered U7. *Geoff Rixon*

An example of one of the first low-floor types in London, dating from 1994, takes up passengers at Beckton bus station in February 2000. The vehicle is SLW24, a Scania N113 with Wright Pathfinder 320 body, working from Upton Park garage on busy route 101, from North Woolwich to Wanstead. *Dave Drury*

Left: On 1 May 1999 Blue Triangle gained route 474, which runs from Canning Town to East Beckton (Asda). The company started the service using Metrobuses and Titans, having placed an order for its first new buses. These were meant to be Volvo B7Ls but, due to delivery delays, Blue Triangle switched to Dennis Tridents with East Lancs Lolyne bodywork. DL905, one of a class of nine, was just two weeks old when photographed at East Beckton. *Geoff Rixon*

Above: Arriva The Shires purchased three Volvo B6BLE vehicles with Wright Crusader bodywork for LTB route H18 when the company took over this service from Metroline, and operates them from Garston garage, Watford. First used on the H18 on 18 November 1999, 3258 was photographed in Kenton Lane, Harrow, on 4 December of that year. *Colin Brown*

Left: Further Metrobus replacements arrived in April 1999 in the form of 20 new Volvo Olympians with Northern Counties Palatine I bodywork. They are operated by First Challenger on route 83 (Ealing Hospital to Golders Green), from Alperton garage. VN95 was photographed in December 1999, passing the Sage old people's home in Golders Green Road. *Dave Brown*

Right: Stagecoach East London's VA76, a Volvo Olympian with Alexander bodywork based at Bow garage, pulls out of Stratford bus station on its way to North Woolwich Free Ferry, on 27 January 2000. *Colin Brown*

Left: Towards the end of 1999, Arriva London South received its first intake of low-floor Alexander-bodied DAFs for routes 68 and X68, operating out of Norwood garage. Compared to earlier members of the DLA class, DLA130 is shorter (10.2m instead of 10.6m) and taller (4.39m instead of 4.2m) and has a forward (instead of central) staircase. This scene is at Elephant & Castle on 2 February 2000. *Geoff Rixon*

Right: The Big Bus Company of Wimbledon has a fleet of over 80 vehicles, the majority of which are former London Transport Fleetlines (DMSs) or Titans. In March 1999, the company began a foreign language service, using Titans with roll-top roofs — a concept reminiscent of the late 1920s/early 1930s when 'all weather' towing coaches (charabancs) were in vogue. The first three Titans were sent to BVG in Berlin for conversion, but kits were then sent over to the UK for subsequent conversions to be carried out here. In this view on Lambeth Bridge, taken on 5 February 2000, Titan OHV 742Y (ex-LT T742) is in 'winter' mode. *Geoff Rixon*

London Central's Bexleyheath Garage has started to receive its new Volvo B7L with Plaxton President bodies for routes 89, 229, 401 and 422. Displacing Leyland Titans in late March 2000, they are 10m in length and have central staircases, and are classified PVL. PVL30 is seen pulling off the stop in Plumstead High Street on route 422 on 8 April 2000. *Geoff Rixon*

The new low-floor B7L chassis from Volvo made its London debut on
1 February 2000 with London Central, carrying Alexander ALX400 bodywork.
Classified AVL, these vehicles operate routes 45 and 63 out of Camberwell and
Peckham garages. AVL25 is seen on route 63, turning into the newly-completed
bus station at Crystal Palace, in February 2000. *Geoff Rixon*

Left: Another new operator, Connex, ventured into bus work in February 2000. The French-owned company, which already ran commuter trains into London from Kent and Sussex, took over route 3 from London Central on re-tendering. Using 29 Dennis Tridents with Alexander bodywork, classified TA, Connex started operations on 5 February. TA22 was photographed crossing Oxford Circus on 12 March. *Geoff Rixon*

Above: Tellings-Golden Miller received nine new Mini Pointer Darts in January 2000 for Hounslow-based routes H20 and H26. Four vehicles for each route received branding on the yellow band; however, the first of the batch remains unbranded as a spare to operate on other routes if required. V301 MDP was caught travelling along Portsmouth Road, Long Ditton, on route 471 (Kingston to Woking) on 8 March 2000. *Geoff Rixon*

Above: Metrobus, now part of Go-Ahead Group, acquired 10 low-floor Optare Excels in 1997 to operate its 358 route between Crystal Palace and Orpington on a 20min frequency. A resplendent P502 OUG lays over at the new Crystal Palace bus station on 26 February 2000. *Geoff Rixon*

Right: In mid-February 2000, First CentreWest's Uxbridge Buses operation began receiving the first of 43 new Dennis Tridents for the very busy Uxbridge to Shepherd's Bush 207 route, upon which they replaced twenty-year-old Metrobuses. Unlike earlier CentreWest deliveries, the new Tridents are long-wheelbase, and their Plaxton President bodies feature forward-mounted staircases. TNL889, one of the first to enter service, is seen on its way to Uxbridge at West Ealing on 11 March 2000. *Geoff Rixon*

Left: London United took delivery of its first low-floor double-deckers in February 2000, in the form of Volvo B7L chassis with Alexander ALX400 bodywork. Eighteen such vehicles are required for the operation of route 220 (Harlesden to Wandsworth) out of Shepherd's Bush garage; these buses are also used on Routemaster route 94 on Sundays. V181 OOE was photographed heading for Wandsworth in Putney Bridge Road on 4 March 2000. *Geoff Rixon*

Above: Wings Buses of Uxbridge started to operate its second route on 1 April 2000, with four new Dennis Dart SLFs with East Lancs Spryte bodies. Registered W435-8 CRN for the new route H50 and funded by Hillingdon Council, it runs between Hayes & Harlington to West Drayton stations carrying Trainlink logos. In doing so it passes through the serene setting of Stockley Business Park, which was the location chosen to take this shot of W436 CRN on Friday 7 April 2000. *Geoff Rixon*

Index of Locations Illustrated